The Impossible

Georges Bataille

THE IMPOSSIBLE

A Story of Rats
followed by
Dianus
and by The Oresteia

Translated by
Robert Hurley

CITY LIGHTS BOOKS
San Francisco

Cover design by Rex Ray

Library of Congress Cataloging-in-Publication Data

Bataille, Georges, 1897–1962.
   [Impossible. English]
   The impossible / by Georges Bataille : translated from
the French by Robert Hurley.
       p.   cm.
   Translation of: L'Impossible.
   ISBN 0-87286-262-3 : $14.95
   I. Title.
   PQ2603.A695I4613   1991
   848'.91209–dc20
                                 91-21312
                                    CIP

CITY LIGHTS BOOKS are edited by Lawrence Ferlinghetti
and Nancy J. Peters and published at the City Lights
Bookstore, 261 Columbus Avenue, San Francisco, CA 94133.

CONTENTS

"His lips kept murmuring 'Jesus!' . . . then, 'Catherine!' As he spoke my name I took his head between my hands, reminding him of the goodness of God and I said to him: 'I wish it!'

. . . .

"When he was buried, my soul reposed in peace and quiet and in such a fragrance of blood that I could not bear the idea of washing away that blood which had flowed from him onto me."

—*Saint Catherine of Siena*

"During this agony, the soul is inundated with inexpressible delights."

—*Saint Teresa of Avila*

PREFACE
TO THE SECOND EDITION

Like the fictional narratives of novels, the texts that follow—the first two at any rate—are offered with the intention of depicting the truth. Not that I'm led to believe they have a convincing quality. I didn't wish to deceive. Moreover there is not in principle any novel that deceives. And I couldn't imagine doing that in my turn better than anyone else. Indeed I think that in a sense my narratives clearly attain the impossible. *To be honest, these evocations have a painful heaviness about them. This heaviness may be tied to the fact that at times horror had a real presence in my life. It may be too that, even when reached in fiction, horror alone still enabled me to escape the empty feeling of untruth . . .*

Realism gives me the impression of a mistake. Violence alone escapes the feeling of poverty of those realistic experiences. Only death and desire have the force that oppresses, that takes one's breath away. Only the extremism of desire and of death enables one to attain the truth.

I first published this book fifteen years ago, giving it an obscure title: The Hatred of Poetry. *It seemed to me that true poetry was reached only by hatred. Poetry had no powerful meaning except in the violence of revolt. But poetry attains this violence only by evoking the* impossible. *Almost no one understood the meaning of the first title, which is why I prefer finally to speak of* The Impossible.

It's true that this second title is far from being clearer.

But it may be one day . . . . : I perceive the course of a convulsion that involves the whole movement of beings. This convulsion goes from death's disappearance to that voluptuous rage which, perhaps, is the meaning of the disappearance.

Humanity is faced with a double perspective: in one direction, violent pleasure, horror, and death—precisely the perspective of poetry—and in the opposite direction, that of science or the real world of utility. Only the useful, the real, have a serious character. We are never within our rights in preferring seduction: truth has rights over us. Indeed, it has every right. And yet we can, and indeed we must, respond to something which, not being God, is stronger than every right, that impossible *to which we accede only by forgetting the truth of all these rights, only by accepting disappearance.*

G.B.

PART ONE

A STORY OF RATS

(Journal of Dianus)

[First Notebook]

Incredible nervous state, trepidation beyond words: to be this much in love is to be sick (and I love to be sick).

B. doesn't cease to dazzle me: the irritation of my nerves makes her even more impressive. Everything about her is extraordinary! But in my trembling I have doubts—she's so facile (She's false, superficial, equivocal . . . Isn't that obvious? She gets muddled and extricates herself more or less, says foolish things haphazardly, lets herself be influenced by fools, and fusses about uselessly, overlooking the crucible, the infinite sieve that I am!).

I know that now I bore her.
Not that I laid myself open to her scorn (I disappoint her in that, out of playfulness, out of kindness, she wanted the impossible from me) but driven as she is, she sets aside what she's already known: what disturbs me about her is this impatience.

I imagine a large nail and her nakedness. Her flame-like movements make me physically dizzy and the nail I drive into her, I can't leave there! As I write, being unable to see her and the hard nail, I dream of clasping her waist: it's not a feeling of happiness but my powerlessness to reach her that stops me: she eludes me in any case, the sickest thing about me being that I want this and I want my love to be necessarily unhappy. Indeed I no longer seek any happiness: I don't want to give it to her, and I want none for myself. I would like always to move her to *anguish* and for her to faint from it: she's the way she is, but I doubt that two beings have ever communicated more deeply in the certainty of their impotence.

In A.'s appartment (I don't know if A. is lying when he says he belongs to the Order of Jesuits: he approached B. in the street, amusing her with his grave hypocrisy; the first day, he put on the cassock at his place and only drank with her), in A.'s apartment, the mixture of an extreme disarray of the senses and an affected elevation of the heart enchants us, it charms us like a liquor.

Often in fact, the three of us laugh like madmen.

What I expect from music: an added degree of depth in that exploration of coldness which is *dark* love (tied to B.'s obscenity and sealed by an endless suffering—a love never violent enough, never shady enough, never close enough to death!).

I differ from my friends in not caring a damn for any convention, taking my pleasure in the basest things. I feel no shame living like a sneaky adolescent, like an old man. Ending up, drunk and red-faced, in a dive full of naked women: to look at me there, sullen, with an anxious curl of the lips, no one would imagine that I am coming. I feel utterly *vulgar* and when I cannot attain my object I at least sink into a real poverty.

I feel dizzy and my head spins. I discover that my "self-confidence" makes me what I am—precisely because it deserts me. If I no longer have my assurance, a void opens up at my feet. The reality of being is the naive certainty of chance, and the chance that elevates me leads me to ruination. I am ashamed to think that I am inferior to the *greatest*: so much so that I never think about it, I forget that others know nothing about me.

The fear that B. will abandon me, leaving me alone and, like an outcast, sick with the desire to lose myself, is finally getting to me. A while ago I wept—or, dry-eyed, accepted the disgust; now day is breaking and the feeling of possible sorrow exhilarates me: life stretches within me like a song modulated in the throat of a soprano.

Happy like a broom whose whirl makes a windmill in the air.

Like a drowning man who goes down clenching his hands, the way one drowns for failing to stretch out one's body as peacefully as in a bed, in the same way . . . but I know.

You're not willing to lose yourself. You will have to come *on your own account*. From anguish you derived pleasures so great—they shook you from head to toe (I mean your sexual joys, your filthy pleasures of the "Moulin Bleu": don't you want to throw in the towel?).

My reply:
"I will give up on one condition . . . "
"What's that?"
"But no . . . I'm afraid of B."

This dreary landscape of windswept mountains, the cold and the melted snow: how I loved living with B. in this uninhabitable place! The weeks went by quickly . . .
In the same circumstances: alcohol, stormy moments (stormy nakedness), painful sleep.

Walking, in a storm, on a dull mountain path is not a relaxation (is more like a reason for being).

What joins me to B. is the impossible, like a void in front of her and me, instead of a secure life together. The lack of a way out, the difficulties recurring in any case, this threat of death between us like Isolde's sword, the desire that goads us to go further than the heart can bear, the need to suffer from an endless laceration, the suspicion even—on B.'s part—that all this will still only lead, haphazardly, to wretchedness, will fall into filth and spinelessness: all this makes every hour a mixture of panic, expectation, audacity, anguish (more rarely, exasperating sensuality), which only action can resolve (but action . . .).

Strange, finally, that the difficulty encountered by vice—paralysis, vice's brake—is due to the feebleness, the wretchedness, of the real possibilities. It is not vice that appalls, but the petty figures that surround it, its puppets, stunted, doltish, bored men and women. To tell the truth I must be for my part a rather desolate mountain to leave the summit accessible even to old ladies in wigs (I almost miss them: in the nightclubs, the clowns, the bad, sickroom smell of gold, the flashy vulgarity are agreeable to me).

I hate those successful beings who lack a sense of limits (of absolute powerlessness): the drunken seriousness of Father A. (he does indeed belong to the Society) is not feigned: his discreet profanities and his behavior correspond—with an indescribable moral severity—to the sense he has of the impossible.

Had dinner yesterday with B. and Father A. Should I attribute the mad pronouncements of A. to the alcohol? or again: might stating the truth be a means of raising doubt and of deceiving more completely?

A. is not diabolical but human (human? wouldn't this be *insignificant?*): if one forgets the robe and the anecdotal interest, the atheist monk serving, he says, a cause hostile to the Church. A Jesuit in a bathrobe (in him the long, bony body and the unctuousness are just another sarcasm) is the most naked man there is: as for his *truth*, B., delighted, touched it . . .

I live in the enchantment of yesterday's dinner: B., beautiful as a she-wolf and wicked, so elegant in a blue and white striped dressing gown, half-open from top to bottom. She sarcastic, too, in the Father's presence and laughing like a darting flame.

These moments of intoxication when we defy everything, when, the anchor raised, we go merrily toward the abyss, with no more thought for the inevitable fall than for the limits given in the beginning, are the only ones when we are completely free of the ground (of laws) . . .
Nothing exists that doesn't have this *senseless sense*—common to flames, dreams, uncontrollable laughter—in those moments when consumption accelerates, beyond the desire to endure. Even utter senselessness ultimately is always this sense made of the negation of all the others. (Isn't this sense basically that of each particular being who, as such, is the *senselessness* of all the others, but only if he doesn't care a damn about enduring—and thought (philosophy) is at the limit of this conflagration, like a candle blown out at the limit of a flame.)

In the face of Father A.'s sharp, cynical, and lucidly narrow logic, B.'s drunken laughter (A. sunk into an armchair—half-naked, B. standing in front of him, derisive and crazy as a flame) was that insensate movement which weighs anchor and sails off naively toward the void. (At the same time my hands were disappearing between her legs . . . blindly those hands searched for the crack, burned themselves in that fire that opens the void to me . . .)

At that moment, the tenderness of nudity (the baring of the legs or the breasts) touched the infinite.

At that moment, desire (the anguish that accompanies friendship) was so wonderfully gratified that I despaired.

That immense moment—like mad laughter, infinitely happy, unmasking what endures after it (by revealing the inevitable decline)—substituted alcohol for water, an absence of death, an endless void, for the apparent nearness of the sky.

A., crafty, inured to the wildest possibilities and disillusioned . . .

If it isn't B., I can't imagine a more ludicrously despairing individual—not from a disappointed hope, but with a true despair. A rigid honesty brought indifferently to bear on tasks that one can't mention without laughing (so subversive and paradoxical are they), a vapidity of methods apparently designed to astonish, a purity in debauchery (the law logically dismissed, he immediately finds himself, for want of preconceptions, on a level with the worst), a mockery aimed at delights going beyond loss of the senses, make A. the analogue of a factory blueprint. Good sense so free of conventions has the obviousness of a mountain— and even its wildness.

B. expresses, in his presence, astonishment at Father A.'s eccentricities.

I point out to her on the other hand what simple

necessities determine his life: the ten years of deep study, the slow apprenticeship in dissimulation, in mental dislocation, make a man impassive. In a slightly changed sense . . . , *perinde ac cadaver.*

"Do you think so?" B. asked (consumed with irony, with pleasure).

Kneeling at the Father's feet . . . herself animally pleased at my folly. Tilted back, our friend's face lit up with a mocking smile.

Not without strain, it relaxed.

The bitter lips and the eyes lost in the depths of the ceiling, swimming with ineffable happiness.

More and more wanton, B. said to me:

"Look at the Reverend's angelic smile."

"The Lord's angels," A. said, "rob the sleep of the just!"

He spoke the way one yawns.

I regret not being dead, looking at B. with her lips wet, and looking into her heart of hearts. To attain exacerbated pleasure, extreme audacity, exhausting the body, the intellect, and the heart all at once, reduces survival almost to nothing. Banishes its peace of mind in any case.

My solitude demoralizes me.

A telephone call from B. forewarns me: I doubt that I shall see her again for a long time.

And "man alone" is damned.

B. and A. live alone, rather willingly. A. in a religious order, B. with her family—however insidious their relations may be with that order, that family.

I shiver with cold. Sudden, unexpected, B.'s departure disheartens me.

I surprise myself: I'm afraid of death—with a fear that is cowardly and childish. I don't care to live unless I'm consumed (otherwise I would have to want to go on). Strange as it may be, my lack of determination to go on takes away my strength to resist: I live drowning in anguish and I'm afraid of death, precisely because I don't care to live.

I can tell that I have the possible toughness within me, the indifference to the worst, the madness it takes in torments: and I tremble nonetheless, I ache.

I know that my affliction is incurable.

Without that she-wolf challenge of B.—lighting up the thickness of the mists like a fire—everything is insipid and space is empty. At this moment, as the sea goes down, life is withdrawing from me.

But if I want to . . .

But no.

I refuse.

I'm assailed by fear in my bed.

That challenge—her lily freshness and the fresh hands of nakedness—like a summit of the heart, inaccessible . . .

But the memory is uncertain.

I remember *badly*, more and more badly.

I am so weak, often, that I lack the strength to write. The strength to lie? I have to say it, too: these words that I string together lie. In prison I wouldn't write on the walls: I would have to tear out my nails searching for the way out.

To write? to turn back one's nails, to hope, utterly in vain, for the moment of deliverance?

My reason for writing is to reach B.

The most disheartening idea: that B. might finally lose the Ariadne's thread which, in the labyrinth of her life, my love for her is.

She knows but forgets (is it not necessary, for that, to forget?) that she and I have entered the darkness of a prison that we will not get out of alive, that we are reduced to pressing, in the cold, the naked heart against the wall, awaiting an ear pressed against the other side.

Damnation! that to reach that moment, prison is necessary, and the darkness, the cold that follow that moment!

Spent an hour yesterday with A.

I want to write this first of all. We don't have the means of reaching at our disposal: to tell the truth, we do reach; we suddenly reach the necessary point and we spend the rest of our lives seeking a lost moment; but how often we miss it, for the precise reason that seeking it leads us away from it. Joining together is doubtless a means . . . of missing the moment of return forever. —Suddenly, in my darkness, in my solitude, anguish gives way to conviction:

it's uncanny, no longer even wrenching (through constant wrenching, it no longer wrenches), *suddenly B.'s heart is in my heart.*

In the course of the conversation, the movement of suffering, like the agitation of a hunted animal, took away my desire to breathe. I was tempted to speak: my temptation was greeted by a mocking face (A. seldom laughs, seldom smiles; in him there is no *lost moment* that he would be condemned to seek: he is *despairing* (like most); usually there remains a lurking thought of accessible happiness.)

Strange reflections, in a cellar-like darkness, of the gleam of nakedness: L.N. and his wife, E., both of them elegant. E. with her back to me, blond, in a pink, low-cut, period dress. She was smiling at me in the mirror. Her insidious gaiety . . . Her husband raises the dress, with the tip of an umbrella, up to her waist.
Très dix-huitième, says N. in bad French. E.'s laughter, in the mirror, had the dizzy malice of alcohol.

Strange that the same senseless gleam shines for every man. Nakedness is frightening: our nature wholly deriving from the scandal in which it has the sense of the horrible . . . What is called *naked* presupposes a lacerated fidelity, is but a shaky, gagged response to the unclearest of calls. The furtive gleam caught sight of in the darkness, does it not demand the giving of a life? Shouldn't each one, defying the hypocrisy of all (such stupidity at the basis of "human" behavior!), rediscover the way that leads him, through flames, to filth, to the darkness of nudity?

The owl flies, in the moonlight, over a field where the wounded cry out.

Like the owl, I fly in the night over my own misfortune.

I am a wretched man, a crippled recluse. I am afraid of death; I love, and, in different ways, I suffer: then I abandon my sorrows *and I say that they lie*. Outside it is cold. I don't know why I am burning in my bed: I have no fire, it's freezing. If I were naked outside, struck down, halted, lost (I would hear better than in my room the whistlings and detonations of bombs—just now the town is being bombed), the chattering of my teeth would still lie.

I undressed so many women at the brothel. I drank, I was intoxicated and was happy only if I was indefensible.

The freedom one has only at the brothel . . .

At the brothel I could take off my pants, sit on the assistant madam's knees and cry. That was of no consequence either, was only a lie, exhausting the miserable possibilities nonetheless.

I have a puerile, honest idea of my rear end, and so much fear at bottom.

A mixture of horror, unhappy love, and lucidity (the owl!) . . .

Like a lunatic escaped from an asylum, my madness at least still confines me.

My delirium is convulsed. I don't know if I laugh at the night, or if the night . . . I am alone, and, without B., I cry out. My cry gets lost in the same way that life is lost in death. Obscenity exacerbates love.

A frightened memory of B. naked under the eyes of A.

I embraced her desperately and our mouths intermingled.

A., excited, kept quiet, "It was like being in church".

And now?

I love B. so much that I love her absence, so much that in her I love my anguish.

My weakness: to burn, to laugh, to exult, but when the cold comes, to lack the courage to live.

The worst: so many indefensible lives—so much vanity, ugliness, and moral emptiness. That woman with the double chin whose immense turban proclaimed the rule of error . . . The crowd—stupidity, failure—on the whole isn't it a mistake? the fall of being in the individual, of the individual in the crowd, isn't it, in our darkness, an "anything rather than"? The worst would be God: rather Madame Charles exclaiming, "My goodness, it's the love of a little darling!"—rather myself in bed with Madame Charles, but the rest of the night sobbing: condemned to want the impossible. In that regard, the tortures, the pus, the sweat, the ignominy.

A whole deathlike activity for paltry results.

In this maze of helplesssness (delusion on all sides), I forget the moment when *the curtain rises* (N. raising the dress, E. laughing in the mirror: I rushed over, took the mouth and the breasts sprang from the dress . . .).

E.'s nakedness . . . , B.'s nakedness, will you deliver me from anguish?
But no . . .
. . . give me more anguish . . .

Extreme devotion is the opposite of piety, extreme vice the opposite of pleasure.

When I think of my mad anxiety, of the need I have to be worried, to be in this world a man breathing uneasily, on his guard, as if he were going to be short of everything, I imagine the horror of my peasant ancestors, eager to tremble with hunger and cold, in the rarefied air of the nights.

How they *demanded*, in the mountain bogs where they lived, to breathe uneasily, to tremble tightly with fear (thinking of food, money, the diseases of animals and men, droughts, selling at a loss) and their vigorous joys at the mercy of prowling ghosts.

As to the inheritance of anguish over nakedness that they bequeathed themselves, the torches bare at the toad moment of conception, nothing more "shameful" of course.

"The fathers ate green grapes and the sons' teeth are on edge."

It makes my skin crawl that my grandmothers have a lump in their throat in me.

Hearing nothing from B., endlessly I follow the path of a dead-drunk blind man, and it seems to me that the whole earth (silent, bored, condemned to a interminable wait) is following it with me.

It is snowing this morning. I am alone and without a fire. The answer would be: the blaze, the warmth of B. But alcohol would fill the glasses, B. would laugh, would talk about A., we would go to sleep, naked as animals, the way the cloud of stars in the sky eludes every conceivable purpose . . .

I receive fine answers, among which the nakedness, the laughter of B. But their meaning scarcely varies. There is not one of them that death does not snatch away in advance. The finest, is it not the coarsest—revealing its poverty of its own accord in a burst of joy—provocative, impotent (as was the nakedness of B. the other night, in front of A.).

B. laughed, facing A., her legs savagely bare to the breasts. Her insolence at such a moment recalled the tortured lovers, spitting their insults into the faces of their tormentors. Isn't this impulse the *freest* (in which the flames in the night shoot up to the clouds)? the most voluptuous? the most insipid? I attempt in writing to capture a reflection of it, but nothing . . . I go into the night without flames and without reflection; everything slips away within me.

Oh, *senseless* sorrow, without regret, without reflection! Here I am, burning with the desire to burn from such agonizing, splintered flames. Between death and physical pain—and pleasure, deeper than death and pain—I drag myself along in a melancholy night, at the edge of sleep.

The powerlessness of memory.—Last year I was going to see the Tabarin show. Eager in advance for the nakedness of the girls (sometimes the colored garter, the garter belt placed on the chair, more rigorously evoke the worst, the naked and desirable flesh—rarely do I see girls on the boards without penetrating their *insipid* intimacy, more deeply than in a bed). I hadn't gone out for months. I went to Tabarin as if I were going to a feast, sparkling with easy lips and sexual parts. In advance, dreaming of the smiling crowd of girls—so beautiful and devoted to the pleasures of nakedness—I drank; a taste of sensual pleasure rose up in me like a sap: I was going to *see* and I was happy in advance. I was drunk as I went inside. From impatience and to be in the first row, I arrived too early (but, exasperating as it is, the wait for the show is enchanting). I had to order, just for myself, a bottle of champagne. In a few minutes I emptied it. The intoxication finally overwhelmed me: when I came out of my stupor *the show was over*, the hall empty and my head even more so. As if I hadn't seen anything. From the beginning to the end, I only had a blank space in my memory.

I left in the blackout. It was as dark inside me as it was in the streets.

I didn't think that night about the memories of my grandparents, whom the marsh mists kept in the mud, their eyes dry and their lips made thinner by anguish. Deriving from the harshness of their circumstances the right to curse others, drawing from their suffering and their bitterness the guiding principle of the world.

My anguish does not come solely from knowing I am free. It requires a possible that *entices* me and frightens me at the same time. The anguish differs from a reasonable fear, in the same way as a fear of heights. The possibility of a fall is disturbing, but the anxiety redoubles if the prospect, instead of repelling, finds an involuntary complicity in the one it frightens: the fascination of vertigo is basically only a desire that is obscurely undergone. The same is true of the excitation of the senses. If one strips naked the part of a pretty young woman going from halfway up the leg to the waist, desire vivifies an image of the possible that nakedness points to. There are those who remain insensible and likewise one is not necessarily subject to vertigo. The pure and simple desire for the abyss is scarcely conceivable; it's aim would be immediate death. But I can love the young woman stripped naked in front of me. If the abyss seems to me to answer my expectations, I immediately dispute the answer, while the lower belly of young women reveals an abysmal aspect only in the long run. It would not be an abyss if it were endlessly available, remaining true to itself, forever pretty, forever stripped naked by desire, and if, for my part, I had inexhaustible strength. But if it does not have the immediately dark character of a ravine, it is no less empty for that and leads to horror nonetheless.

I am gloomy this evening: my grandmother's joy in pursing her lips in the mud, my damnable meanness toward myself, and that is what is left to me of the other night's pleasures (of the beautiful open dressing gown, of the void between the legs, of the defiant laughs).

I should have known that B. would be afraid.
Now I'm afraid in my turn.

Telling the story of the rats, how could I have misjudged the horror of the situation, the extent of it?
(The Father laughed, but his eyes dilated. I told the two stories one after the other:

X. (dead for twenty years, he is the only writer of our time who dreamed of equaling the wealth of the *Thousand and One Nights*) occupying a hotel room where men dressed in different uniforms (dragoon, fireman, sailor, military police, delivery man . . .) would be shown in. A lace cover would conceal X., stretched out on the bed. The role-players would walk about in the room without saying a word. A young elevator man, loved by X., would arrive last, dressed in the finest uniform and carrying a cage wherein lived a rat. Setting the cage on a pedestal table, the elevator operator would arm himself with a hat pin with which he would pierce the rat. At the moment when the pin penetrated the heart, X. would soil the lace cover.

X. would also go to a basement brothel in the Saint-Séverin district.

"Madame," he would say to the proprietress, "do you have any rats today?"

The proprietress would answer as X. expected.

"Yes, Monsieur," she would say, "we have rats."

"Ah . . . "

"But, Madame," X. would continue, "are *these rats* nice ones?"

"Yes, Monsieur, very nice rats."

"Really? but these rats . . . are they big?"

"You'll see, they're enormous rats."

"Because I need huge rats, you understand . . . "

"Ah, Monsieur, giants . . . "

X. would then pounce on an old prostitute who was waiting for him.)

I told my story in the end the way it must be told.

A. got up and said to B.:

"What a shame, my dear friend, you are so young."

"I'm sorry too, Father."

"For lack of magpies, right?"

(Even the . . . . of elegant personages has the hugeness of a rat.)

This is not exactly to fall into a void: as the fall extracts a scream, a flame rises up . . . , but the flame is like a scream, is not graspable.

The worst is no doubt a relative duration, giving the illusion that one grasps, that one will grasp at least. What remains in our hands is the woman and there is the choice of two things, either she escapes us or the fall into the void that love is escapes us: we are reassured in the latter case, but like dupes. And the best that can happen to us is to have to search for the lost moment (when secretly, perhaps even with happiness, but ready to die of it, we gave our only scream).

A child's scream, a cry of terror and yet of intense happiness.

Those rats that come out of our eyes as if we dwelled in tombs . . . : A. himself has the dash and character of a rat— all the more alarming because one doesn't know where he comes from nor where he makes off to.

That part of the young woman between the mid-leg and the waist—which emphatically answers one's expectations—answers like the elusive transit of a rat. What fascinates us is vertiginous: sickly smells, recesses, the sewer, have the same *illusory* essence as the void of a ravine into which one is about to fall. The void also attracts me, otherwise I wouldn't have any vertigo—but I will die if I fall, and what can I do with a void—except fall into it? If I survived the fall I would confirm the inanity of desire—as I've done countless times with the "little death."

Unfailingly, instantly, the "little death" exhausts desire (does away with it) and puts us in the state of a man at the edge of a ravine, tranquil, indifferent to the sorcery of the void.

Comical that A. and B. and I, stretched out together, debated the most distant political questions—at night, in the relaxation that followed satisfaction.

I was caressing B.'s head.

A. was holding B.'s foot in his hand—she showing no regard for elementary decency.

We broached metaphysics.

We rediscovered the tradition of the dialogues!

Might I write that dialogue? I drop the idea for now, I'm getting irritable.

Too much anguish (due to B.'s absence).

I'm struck by this: reporting that dialogue here, I would abandon the pursuit of desire.

But no, at the moment desire blinds me.

The way a dog gnaws a bone . . .

Might I give up my unhappy search?

It must also be said: life is more mobile than language—even mad language—when the most strained language is not the most mobile (I joke endlessly with B.; we are rivals in laughing at one another: in spite of my concern with being truthful, I can't say any more about this. I write the way a child cries: a child slowly relinquishes the reasons he has for being in tears).

Might I lose my reasons for writing?

And even . . .

If I spoke of war, of torture . . . : seeing that war and torture, today, are situated at points which ordinary language has determined, I would stray from my object—which draws me beyond the accepted limits.

In this way I see, too, how philosophical reflection betrays, for it cannot come up to one's expectations, having only a limited object—which is defined in terms of another, defined in advance—so that compared with the object of desire it is never anything but a matter of indifference.

Who would refuse to see that, in the guise of frivolity, my object is what matters, that others regarded as the most serious are really just the means leading to the expectation of mine? Freedom is nothing if it is not the freedom to live at the edge of limits where all comprehension breaks down.

The other night's nakedness is the only point of application of my thought that finally leaves it faltering (from the excess of desire).

B.'s nakedness calls *my expectation* into question, when that expectation alone is capable of questioning *that which is* (the expectation wrenches me away from the *known*, for the lost *moment* is lost forever; under the cover of the *déjà vu*, I search avidly for what lies beyond it: the *unknown*).

What does philosophy matter since it is this naive contestation: the questioning that we can only undertake when we are *appeased*! how could we be appeased if we did not rely on a whole body of presupposed knowlege? Introducing a metaphysical given at the extreme limit of thought comically reveals its essence: that of every philosophy.

As for that dialogue, only the breakdown that follows . . . made it possible.

How exasperating it is to be able to speak only when *appeased* by *war* (appeased, eager for peace), so that thinking it through, I write this book, which appears to be by an impartial blind man.

(To speak of war in the usual way requires that one forget the fundamental impossible. The same is true of philosophy. One can't face things without slackening— even to fight and get ourselves killed diverts us from the impossible.)

When I glimpse, as I do today, the *simple* bottom of things (that which, provided an infinite good fortune, agony will fully reveal), I know that I should keep silent: by speaking, I postpone the moment of the irremediable.

I just received these simple words from B., postmarked at V. (a little town in the Ardéche), written in a childish hand (after six days of silence):

Slightly injured, I'm writing with my left hand.
Scenes from a bad dream.
Adieu.
Hug the Reverend all the same.

B.

What's the point of going on?
Continue the losing game?
No reason to write or to go this evening to the station. Or this one: I would rather spend the night in a train, preferably in third class. Or this: if like last year the gamekeeper of B.'s estate beats me up in the snow, I know someone who will laugh.

Me naturally!

I should have guessed. B. has taken refuge with her father . . .

I'm discouraged.

B. runs away from me, takes refuge where I can't reach her in any way, even though that drunk of an old man beats her (her father: that old fool jabbering about accounts), even though she had promised . . . I feel worse and worse.

I laughed, I laughed alone. I got up hissing and let myself fall to the floor, as if, at one go, I had hissed away the little strength that I have left. And I wept on the carpet.

B. is running away from herself. And yet . . .

No one has challenged fate the way she has (with A.).

I know very well: she didn't give this any thought. While I myself am aware (so much so and how painful the awareness is! an awareness puffed out like a cheek! but how can I be surprised that B. would run away from me!).

My temples are still throbbing. Outside, the snow is falling. It's been falling for several days apparently. I'm feverish and I hate this blaze; for several days my loneliness has been truly insane. Now even the room lies: as long as it was cold and without a fire I kept my hands under the covers and I was less harried, my temples throbbed less. In a half-sleep, I dreamed I was dead: the coldness of the room was my casket, the houses of the town other tombs. I got used to it. I felt a certain pride in being unhappy. I trembled, without hope, undone like flowing sand.

Absurdity, boundless impotence: sick, a few steps from B. in this small town inn, without any way of reaching her.

Would she write to me on finding in Paris the address of the hotel at V.?

She wouldn't want to interfere with bad luck, I imagine.

Decided, several times, to send her a note.

It's doubtful whether she would come and even whether she could (everything gets known in little towns). I calculate endlessly; it's certain that Edron (the gamekeeper-caretaker) would intercept the note and give it to the father. There would be a knock at my door and, like last year, it wouldn't be B., but little Edron (a tiny old man, quick as a rat) who would fall upon me and, like last year, beat me to the ground with his walking stick. The finishing touch is that today, no longer capable of being surprised, I still wouldn't be able to do anything. In my bed, I don't have the least bit of strength.

Oh bogus Don Juan in his frigid inn, victim of the commander's caretaker!

Last year, it was in the snow, at the crossroads where I was waiting for B.: he lunged forward; I didn't understand that he was attacking me, I did understand receiving a big blow on the head. I blacked out and came to under the old man's kicks. He was hitting me in the face. I was covered with blood. He didn't push it any further and left running the way he had come.

Raised up on my hands, I watched my blood run. From my nose and lips onto the snow. I got up and pissed in the sun. I was in pain, cramped by the wounds. I was nauseous and, no longer having any means of reaching B., I entered into this darkness where, ever since, I plunge deeper every hour and lose myself a little more.

I am calm (more or less) if I reflect: little Edron is not the cause of it, I *never* have any means of reaching B. B. eludes me in every way, appearing as suddenly as Edron, disappearing just as suddenly. I wanted the hotel, its lack of an exit, this vain anteroom of the void. I don't know if I'm going to die (perhaps?), but I can no longer imagine a better comedy of death than my stay at V.

My teeth chatter, I shiver with fever, and I laugh. My burning hand shaking the icy hand of the Commander, I imagine him in my hand, changed into a notary's clerk, bald, little, flat as a piece of paper. But my laugh sticks in my throat: he drinks and beats his daughter. B., anxious to hold her own against them, for weeks at his mercy! And her mother is ill . . . : he treats her like a whore in front of the maids! But I'm losing my mind, while he's beating his daughter and will kill her.

"The truth is, the actor didn't care about B. One couldn't even say exactly that he loved her. His so-called love had no meaning apart from the anguish he drew from it. What he loved was the night. He preferred B. to other women, because she evaded him, fled from him, and, during her long flights, was under threats of death. He loved the night, truly, like a lover loves the woman of his life."

Not at all. B. herself is the night, yearns for the night. I will let go of this world one day: then the night will be the night, I will die. But being alive, what I love is the love that life has for the night. It's fitting that my life, since it has the necessary strength, is the anticipation of an object leading it toward the night. We toil vainly in search of happiness: the night itself demands from us the strength to love it. If we live on, we must find the necessary strength—which we'll have to spend out of love for it.

When I left Paris I cut the bridges behind me. My life at V., from the outset, was no longer different from a bad dream; only the absurdity of it remained: my luck was to be sick, in unbearable circumstances.

A letter was forwarded to me from Paris: my sadness is so great that that at certain moments I take to moaning out loud.

The letter is, like the first note, written with the left hand, but less undecided:

". . . my father," she says, "dragged me across the rooms by the hair. I screamed—that hurts like hell. My mother very nearly put her hand over my mouth. He will kill us, my mother and me, he says, and he'll kill you next, because he sneers that he doesn't want to make you unhappy! He took one of my fingers and forced it back with such a diabolical meanness that he broke the bone. And I couldn't have imagined such a violent pain. I don't quite understand what happened: I screamed, with the window open, just as a flock of crows was passing; their cries blended with mine. Maybe I'm going crazy.

"He is suspicious of you: he goes into the hotels at meal time, passing through the dining room. He's insane: the doctor wants to confine him, but his wife, who's as crazy as we are, won't hear of it . . . You're on his mind from morning to night: *he hates you above all else.* When he speaks of you he puts out a little red tongue from his frog-like head.

"I don't know why, but at all hours of the day he calls you 'my lord' and 'crocodile.' He says you will marry me, because he says you want the fortune, the castle: we shall have a 'funeral wedding' "!

No doubt about it, I'm going mad myself here in my room.

I'll go to the castle through the snowstorm, shivering in my overcoat. At the door of the entrance gate old Edron will appear. I'll see his spiteful, furious mouth and I won't hear his abuse, drowned out by the noise of the barking!

I curled up in my bed and cried.

Crocodile tears!

She, B., doesn't cry, has never cried.

I imagine her in one of the hallways of the castle, like a current of air, slamming the doors one after the other, and laughing, in spite of everything, about my crocodile tears.

It's still snowing.

My heart beats more violently if I hear footsteps in the hotel: B. going to general delivery would find my letters there and would come?

Someone knocked and I no longer doubted that she had come, that the wall separating me from her would open . . . I already imagined that fleeting pleasure: seeing her again, after so many days and nights. Father A. opened the door, a slight smile, a strange mocking look in his eyes.

"I've heard from B.," he said. "I've finally received a note asking me to come. She says there's nothing you can do. Me, my robe . . . "

I begged him to go immediately to the castle.

He saw me thin and haggard beneath an eight-day beard.

"What's the matter with you? I'll give her your news."

"I'm sick," I told him. "I haven't been able to let her know. The news that I have is older than yours."

I described the state I was in.

"Where was it," I continued, "that I read this phrase: *This cassock is undoubtedly a bad omen*"? I imagine the worst.

"Don't worry," he said, "I've spoken about you in the hotel. A misfortune is quickly made known in a little town."

"The castle is far from here?"

"Three kilometers. B. was definitely alive a few hours ago. We never know more than that. Let me rekindle your fire, it's cold as an ice pack in your room."

I knew she wouldn't go to general delivery!

And now?

My messenger is hurrying through the snow: he resembles those crows whose cries blended with those of B. in her room.

Those birds flying over the snows are probably accompanying the Jesuit, going towards the room where B. cried out. At the same time I imagine B.'s nakedness (the breasts, the hips, the fur), the torturer's toad face, the red tongue: and now, the crows, the priest.

I feel my heart slowly stirred, to the point where one touches the intimacy of things.

A. scurries like a rat!

My disorderly behavior, the window looking onto the void and my exasperating "No matter!", as if I were gripped, harrassed by the weather, on the eve of gruesome events . . .

As if the meeting at the father's castle (of the daughter, my mistress, and her lover, the Jesuit) gave my pain some imperceptible extravagance . . .

. . . .
. . . . what dawn is breaking in
me? what inconceivable light? illuminating the snow, the
cassock, the crows . . .

. . . so much cold, pain, and obscenity! but that rigorous
clockwork (the priest), suited for the most delicate missions,
obliged to walk with his teeth chattering! . . .

. . . I don't know what is turning in my head—in the
clouds—like an impalpable grinding wheel—dazzling—
boundless void, bitterly cold, yielding a pure weapon . . .

. . . oh, my sickness, what an chilling exaltation, tanta-
mount to a murder . . .
. . . henceforth I have no more limits: what grinds in the
emptiness within me is a consuming pain from which there
is no escape short of dying . . .
. . . B.'s cry of pain, the earth, the sky and the cold are
naked like bellies in love-making . . .

. . . .
. . . .
. . . .
. . . .
. . . . A., his teeth chattering on the threshold, hurls himself at B., strips her naked, tears off her clothes in the cold. At that moment the father arrives (not Father A. but the father of B.), the weasel-faced little man, beaming like a fool, saying softly:"I knew it, it's a farce!" . . . .
. . . .
. . . . the little man, the father, creeps up, jeering, and straddles the mad couple on the threshold (spread out on the snow, and next to them— bearing in mind the cassock, and above the all *the sweat of death*—shit would look pure to me): he cups his hands (the father, his eyes glittering with spite) and cries in a low voice: "Edron!" . . . .
. . . .
. . . . something bald and mustached, with the crafty movements of a burglar, a soft, patently false, sweet chuckle: he calls out in a low voice: "Edron! the shotgun!" . . . .
. . . .
. . . . in the sleepy silence of the snow, an explosion resounds . . . .
. . . .
. . . .

I wake up a little uneasy and yet cheerful.

The oblique sides of being, by which it escapes the meager simplicity of death usually reveal themselves only to cold lucidity: only the cheerful malice of indifference reaches those distant limits where even the tragic is unpretentious. It is just as tragic, but it is not ponderous. It's stupid at bottom that we usually accede to those disconcerting regions only in a contracted state.

It's strange that A., he who . . . , guided me in my dreamlike actions.

In this suspended moment, when even the idea of B.'s death leaves me indifferent, I still don't doubt that if I hadn't loved her as I do, I couldn't have known my condition.

Regardless of the reason, A. helped me a good deal in one year to pose, lucidly, those problems imposed on life by the poverty of reflection ("poverty" is easily said, when the meaning of rich and poor is given in reflection!). The empty lucidity of A., the contempt he has for that which it isn't, flowed into me like the wind into a shack with empty windows. (It's true, I'm obliged to state this qualification: A. would scoff at this comparison which immediately shows contempt's lack of self-confidence.)

A.'s inanity: to be without desire (no longer to expect anything). Lucidity excludes desire (or perhaps kills it, I don't know): as for what remains, he controls it, while I . . .

But what am I to say, in fact, about myself? At this extreme, exhausting moment I can imagine that I let desire become exacerbated in order to find that last moment, when the greatest light imaginable illuminates what is rarely seen by the eyes of men, darkness illuminating the light!

I am so tired! How did I write these ambiguous sentences, when each thing is given simply? Darkness is the same thing as light . . . , but no. The truth is, nothing can be said about the state I'm in other than that's that.

It's bizarre: the elements subsist in a comical light: I can still distinguish them and see them as comical, but as a matter of fact, the comical goes so far that one can't talk about it.

A complete accord is reached by what cannot by any means reach an accord: in this new light, the discord is greater than it ever was. Love for B. makes me laugh at her death and her pain (I don't laugh at any other death) and the purity of my love undresses her down to the shit.

The idea that Father A., a while ago, was half-dead with

cold coming to my assistance. He's hard to discompose. It's a shame.

Obviously I doubt whether I wanted . . . I've suffered. My current state, marked by a keen lucidity, is the effect of an exaggerated anguish. Which I know will start again later.

A.'s lucidity depends on a lack of desire. Mine is the result of an excess—undoubtedly it is also the only true lucidity. If it is only the negation of delirium, lucidity is not completely lucid, is still a bit the fear of going all the way— transposed into boredom, that is, into contempt for the object of an excessive desire. We reason with ourselves and we tell ourselves: this object doesn't have *in itself* the value that desire gives it. We don't see that mere lucidity, which we also attain, is still blind. We must see at the same time the delusion *and the truth* of the object. No doubt we have to know that we are deluding ourselves, that the object is first of all what is perceived by a desireless being, but *it is* also what a desire perceives in it. B. *is* also what is only attained by the extremity of delirium and my lucidity would not exist if my delirium were not so great. Just as it would not exist if the other, ridiculous sides of B. escaped me.

Day is falling, the fire is dying, and I'll soon have to stop writing, obliged by the cold to retract my hands. With the curtains drawn aside, I can make out the silence and the snow through the window panes. Under a low sky, this infinite silence weighs on me and frightens me. It lies heavy like the intangible presence of bodies laid out in death.

I imagine this padded silence alone measures up to an immensely tender, but entirely free, wonderstruck and defenseless, exhaltation. When M. lay before me in death, lovely and oblique like the silence of the snow, unobtrusive like it but, like it, like the cold, mad with exacerbated rigor, I already knew this immense tenderness, which is only the last degree of sorrow.

. . . how great is the silence of death in the recollection of debauchery, when debauchery itself is the freedom of death! how great is the love in debauchery! the debauchery in love!

. . . if now I think—at this most far away moment of a breakdown, a physical and moral disgust—of the pink tail of a rat in the snow, it seems to share *in the intimacy* of "that which is"; a slight uneasiness clutches my heart. And certainly I know that the intimacy of M., who is dead, was like the tail of a rat, *lovely as the tail of a rat!* I knew already that the intimacy of things is death.

. . . and naturally, *nakedness is death*—and the more truly "death" the lovelier it is!

The anguish has slowly returned, after that brief spell of immense tenderness . . .

It is late. A. doesn't return. He should at least have telephoned, notified the hotel.

The thought of a finger deliberately broken, by the madman . . .

This delay, this silence, my waiting, open the door to fear. It's been dark for hours. In the long run the composure that I usually have, even during the unpleasant hours of anguish, abandons me. Like a bitter challenge, the memory comes back to me of what a prostitute told me one day (she was having a session with me): her employer boasted of having, in July 1914, stockpiled thousands of widows' veils.

The horrible wait for what doesn't come, the widow's wait, irremediably a widow already, but with no way of knowing, living on hope. Each additional moment that marks the accelerated beats of the heart tells me it's foolish to hope (we had agreed that A. would telephone if he wasn't coming back).

No more question of my indifference to B.'s death, except that I tremble at having felt it.

I get lost in conjectures, but the evidence grows.

$\big[$*Second Notebook*$\big]$

The hope for a telephone disturbance: I got up, covered myself with an overcoat, went downstairs: the feeling, in the back of the lobby, of being—at last—beyond human limits, exhausted, with no return imaginable. I literally trembled. Now, remembering that I trembled, I feel reduced, in this world, to that trembling, as if my whole life had no other meaning than my cowardice.

The cowardice of a half-bearded man, wandering, ready to weep, through the icy corridors of a station hotel and having a hard time distinguishing between the clinical lights (nothing real any more) and the definitive darkness (death), reduced in this world to that trembling.

The ringing of the telephone went on so long that I imagined the whole château already in the grip of death. A woman's voice finally answered. I asked for A.

"He's not here," the voice said.

"What?" I shouted. I insisted, speaking intelligibly.

"The gentleman is perhaps somewhere else."

I protested.

"Somewhere else in the house," said the voice, "but the gentleman is not in the office."

She resumed in an unexpected tone, neither too stupid, nor clever:

"There are things happening at the castle."

"Please, madame," I begged, "this gentleman is undoubtedly there. If he is still alive, tell him that someone is calling him."

This was answered by a stifled laugh, but the kind voice conceded:

"Yes, monsieur. I'll go look for him."

I heard the receiver being put down and even the sound of footsteps receding. Someone closed the door and then nothing.

At the height of exasperation, I seemed to hear a call and a noise like dishes breaking. The unbearable wait continued. After an endless time, I no longer doubted that the connection had been cut. I hung up and asked for the number again but was told, "The line is busy." At the sixth try the operator said:

"Please don't try again, there's no one on the line."

"What?" I shouted.

"The receiver is off the hook, but nobody is talking. Nothing can be done. They must have forgotten it."

Useless in fact to keep on trying.

I stood up in the booth and groaned:

"Wait all night . . . "

No longer the shadow of a hope, but I was dominated by the idea of knowing at all costs.

Returning to my room, I remained frozen and huddled on a chair.

I got up finally. I was so weak that dressing myself was incredibly difficult: I wept from the effort.
On the stairs I had to stop and lean against the wall.

It was snowing. I had the station buildings in front of me, a gas refinery cylinder. Suffocated, mangled by the cold, I walked in the virgin snow. My pace in the snow and my shivering (my teeth were chattering feverishly) were utterly futile.

Drawn into myself, I voiced a tremulous " . . . oh . . . oh . . . oh." It was in the nature of things: should I persist in the undertaking, lose myself in the snow? This project had only one justification: what I absolutely refused was to wait and I had chosen. It so happened, it was my luck, that this particular day there was only one way to avoid waiting.

"So," I told myself (I don't know whether I was over-come: the difficulties were bringing me relief finally), "the only thing left for me to do is beyond my strength."

I thought:
"Precisely because it's beyond my strength, and what's more it can't succeed in any case—the caretaker, the dogs . . .—I cannot abandon it."

The wind-driven snow lashed my face, blinding me. My curse was raised in the darkness against a doomsday silence.
I groaned like a madman in this solitude:
"My sorrow is too great!"
My voice called out shakily.

I heard the crunching of my shoes: the snow erased my tracks as I advanced, as if, clearly, there was no question of going back.

I went forward in the night: the idea that behind me the bridges were cut soothed me. It reconciled my state of mind with the severity of the cold! A man came out of a cafe and disappeared in the snow. Noticing the lighted interior, I headed for the door and opened it.

I made the snow fall from my hat.

I went over to the stove: at that moment I decided it wasn't good to feel how much I liked the heat of a stove.

"That being the case," I said to myself, laughing inside with a dull chuckle, "I shall not return: I shall not leave!"

Three railroad workers were playing bar billiards.

I asked for a grog. The proprietress poured the brandy into a little glass, then emptied it into a big one. I got a large amount: she started laughing. I wanted some sugar and to obtain it I tried a crude joke. She laughed loudly and sugared the hot water.

I felt degraded. The joke made me the accessory of those people who expected nothing. I drank that steaming grog. In my overcoat I had some tablets for the flu. I remembered they contained caffeine and I swallowed several.

I was unreal, light.

Next to a game in which rows of colored football players confronted each other.

The alcohol and the caffeine stimulated me: I was alive.

I asked the proprietress for the address of . . .

I paid and left the place.

Outside I took the road to the castle.

The snow had stopped falling, but the air was frigid. I walked against the wind.

I was now taking the step that my ancestors had not been able to take. They lived next to the bog where at night the cruelty of the world, the cold, the frost, sustained their bitter character: avarice, toughness in the face of excessive suffering. My exasperated entreaty, my expectation, were just as linked to the nature of the night but I was no longer resigned: my hypocrisy did not change this ludicrous condition into a test willed by God. I was going to pursue my mania for questioning to the end. This world had given me—and taken away—WHAT I LOVED.

How I suffered by going out into that immensity before me: it was no longer snowing, the wind was raising the snow. In places the snow came up to my calves. I had to climb an interminable slope. The icy wind filled the air with such a tension, such a rage that it seemed my temples would burst, my ears bleed. No way out imaginable— except for the castle . . . where Edron's dogs . . . death . . . I walked, in these circumstances, with the energy of delirium.

Obviously I was suffering, but I was aware that in a sense this excess of suffering was voluntary. No connection with the suffering, *undergone* without recourse, of the prisoner being tortured, of the deportee prostrated by hunger, of fingers that are only a salt-freshened wound. In this rage of cold, I was mad. What lies within me in the way of senseless energy was strained to the breaking point—I seem to have laughed, deep down, biting my sad lips—laughed, no doubt, while crying out, at B. Who knows B.'s limits better than I?

But—will they believe me?—the suffering naively sought, B.'s limits, only sharpened my pain; in my simplicity, my tremors opened me to that silence that extends farther than conceivable space.

I was far, so far from the world of calm reflections, my

unhappiness had that empty, electric sweetness which is like fingernails that are turned back.

I reached the limits of exhaustion, my strength abandoned me. The cold had the impossible, senselessly strained cruelty of a battle. Too far to return, would it be long before I fell? I would remain inert and the snow, which the wind was blowing, would cover me. I would soon die once fallen. Unless I arrived first at the castle . . . (Now I laughed at them, at those people of the castle: they would do what they pleased with me . . .). In the end I was weak, incredibly so, advancing more and more slowly, lifting my feet from the snow only with great difficulty, in the state of an animal that froths, fights to the end, but is reduced, in the darkness, to a miserable death.

I wanted nothing more than to know—perhaps with my frozen hands to touch a body (my hand so cold already that it could join with hers)—the cold that was cutting my lips was like the rage of death: it was the fact of breathing it in, of desiring *it*, that transfigured those painful moments. I rediscovered in the air, around me, that eternal, senseless reality which I had known only once, in the room of a dead woman: *a kind of suspended leap.*

In the dead woman's room there was a stony silence, pushing back the limits of the sobs, as if, the sobs no longer having an end, the whole rent world let one glimpse the infinite terror through the opening. Such a silence is beyond sorrow: the silence is nothing of course; it even conjures away the conceivable responses and holds every possibility suspended in the complete absence of tranquillity.

How *sweet* terror is!

Unimaginable, basically, the lack of suffering and the skin-deep nature of sorrow, the lack of reality, the dream-like consistency of the horrible. Yet I was *in the suspense of death*.

What do we know by dint of living if the death of the beloved does not usher in horror (emptiness) at the very point where we cannot bear for it to enter: but then we know what door the key opens.

How *changed* the world is! how beautiful it was, bathed in a halo of lunar light! In the very bosom of death, M. exhaled *in its sweetness* a holiness that caught my throat. The fact that before dying she became depraved, but like a child—in that bold and desperate way, which is doubtless a sign of holiness (which gnaws and consumes the body)—finished giving her anguish a sense of excess—of a leap beyond the bounds.

What death transfigured, my sorrow reached like a cry.

I was torn apart and my brow was frozen—from an inner and painful sort of frost—the stars revealed at the zenith between the clouds made my pain complete: I was naked, defenseless in the cold; in the cold my head was bursting. It no longer mattered whether I fell, whether I continued to suffer in the extreme, whether I died. At last I saw the dark mass—*no lights*—of the castle. The night swooped down on me like a bird on its miserable prey; the cold suddenly spread to my heart: I would not reach the castle . . . which death inhabited; but death . . .

Those crows on the snow, in the sun, whose flying throngs I see from my bed, whose calls I hear from my room, could they be?

. . . the same ones—that answered B.'s cry when her father . . . ?

How surprised I was waking up in that sunlit room, cozy from the heat of the stove! The crimps, the stresses, the fractures of pain, persisting like a habit, still connected me to anguish, which nothing around me justified any longer. I hung on, the victim of a bad turn: "Remember your wretched situation," I told myself. I got up painfully, I suffered, shaking on my legs. I slipped, leaning on the table—a medicine bottle fell and broke. It was nice and warm but I was trembling, oddly dressed in a shirt that was too short, its front tail coming up to my navel.

B. dashed in and shouted:

"Maniac! back to bed quick! no, wait . . . ," stammering, shouting.

The way a crying baby, suddenly seized with a desire to laugh, wants to go on suffering but can't . . . , I pulled at the tail of the little shirt, I was trembling with fever and, laughing in spite of myself, I couldn't keep the shirttail from rising . . . B. flew into a temper but I noticed that in that fury she was laughing . . .

She was obliged (I asked her to, unable to wait any longer) to leave me alone for a moment (it was less awkward for her to be overcome out of my presence, to go and pace the emptiness of the corridors for a short while). I thought of the *dirty* habits of lovers. I was exhausted but cheerfully so; the endless time which the details of the operation required exasperated me, amused me. I had to put off for a few minutes my eagerness to *know*. Letting myself go, forgetting myself, like a dead man, inert in my sheets, the question "What is happening?" had the gaiety of a slap in the face.

I clung to the last possibility for anguish.
B. asked me timidly, "Are you better?". Answering her with "Where am I?," I let myself resort to that fixed sort of panic which the eyes express by opening wide.
"In the house," she said.
"Yes," she continued, sheepish. "In the castle."
"But . . . your father?"
"Don't worry about that."
She looked like a child who's done something wrong.
"He's dead," she explained after moment had passed.
She let the words drop quickly, with her head bowed . . .

(The telephone scene became clear. I found out later that, shouting, sobbing: "Please, madame," I had made a little girl of ten laugh.)

No doubt about it, B.'s eyes were avoiding mine.

"Is he here . . . ?" I asked.
"Yes."

She cast a furtive glance.
Our eyes met: she had a smile at the corners of her mouth.
"How was I found?"
B. looked positively taken aback. It was her desperation that made her say:
"I asked the Reverend, 'Why is there a hump in the snow?' "
In a sick person's cracked voice I insisted:
"Where exactly?"
"On the road, at the entrance to the castle drive."
"You carried me?"
"The Reverend and I."
"What were you doing, the Reverend and you?"
"Don't be upset any more; you should let me talk now, without interrupting . . . We left the house around ten. We ate dinner first, A. and I (Mother didn't want to have dinner). I did my best but it was hard for us get away. Who could have known how crazy you would become?"
She placed her hand on my forehead. It was the left hand (It seemed to me at that moment that everything was going wrong; she had her right hand in a scarf).
She continued, but her hand was trembling.

"We were barely late: if you had only waited for us . . . "
I groaned feebly:
"I didn't know anything."

"The letter was rather clear . . . "
I was astonished: I learned that a letter given to the doctor should have reached the hotel before seven o'clock.

A. announced the father's death, telling me that he would be coming back late and that B. would accompany him.

I said to B. in a soft voice:
"No one delivered any letter to the hotel." (In actual fact, he felt so cold that he got drunk; he forgot the letter in his pocket.)

B. took my hand in her left hand, "gauchely" interlacing her fingers with mine.
"If you didn't know anything you should have waited. Edron would have let you die! and you didn't even make it to the house!"

When B. discovered me I had just fallen. My body was completely covered with a thin layer of snow. The snow would have quickly killed me if, contrary to all expectations, someone, B., had not turned up.

B. drew her right hand out of the scarf, joined it to the left and I saw that despite the plaster cast she was trying to wring her hands.

"Did I hurt you?" I asked.

"I can no longer imagine . . . "

She fell silent, but she continued to move her hands restlessly on her dress. She resumed speaking:

"Do you remember, at the junction where you fell, coming from the castle you go through a grove of little pines where the road starts to wind up the hill? You reach the saddle at the highest place. Just when I was about to notice the hump, the wind took hold of me, I wasn't dressed warmly enough, I had to stop myself from crying out, even A. began to groan. At that moment I looked at the house, which you look down on from there—I thought of death and remembered that he had twisted my . . . "

She fell silent.

She was painfully absorbed in her thoughts.

After a long while, her head low, continuing a difficult twisting movement of her hands, she spoke again—rather softly:

" . . . as if the wind had the same hostility as he."

Despite the prostration of my physical suffering, I wished with all my strength that I could help her. I understood at that moment that the "hump" and my inanimate body—which were not in any way distinguishable from a corpse—represented in that darkness a greater cruelty than her father's or than the cold . . . It was hard for me to bear that terrible language—which love had found.

We finally extricated ourselves from these heavy reflections.

She smiled:

"You remember my father?"

" . . . such a little man . . . "

" . . . so comical . . . He was mad; everything would tremble in his presence. He would break everything in such a absurd way . . . "

"It makes you tremble?"

"Yes . . . "

She fell silent but didn't stop smiling.

She said finally:

"He's there . . . "

She pointed with her eyes.

"Hard to say what he looks like . . . a toad—that has just

swallowed a fly . . . How ugly he is!"

"You're fond of him—still . . . ?"

"He fascinates."

Someone knocked.

Father A. swiftly crossed the room.

He doesn't have that nullified look of clergymen. His bearing reminds me of large, lean birds of prey that I saw at the Anvers zoo.

He came to the foot of the bed, wordlessly exchanging looks with us; B. could not hold back a smile of complicity.

"Everything works out, in the end," said A.

State of exhaustion. A. and B., next to the bed, like haystacks in a field, on which the sun fixes its last rays.

A feeling of dreaming, sleeping. I must have spoken but my unfaithful memory withheld from me what at all costs I must have said. Inwardly tense, but I had forgotten.

A painful, irremediable feeling, linked to the roaring of the fire.

B. put in more wood and slammed the stove door.

A. and B. on a chair, an armchair. A dead man a little further away in the house.

A. with his long birdlike profile, hard, useless, "deconsecrated church."

The doctor called back for me apologized for forgetting the letter the day before; found that I had congestion of the lungs—a mild case.

On all sides, oblivion . . .

I imagined that little dead man in the state room, with his gleaming cranium. Night was falling—outside, the clear sky, the snow, the wind. Now the peaceful boredom, the pleasantness of the room. My distress *finally* boundless, precisely in that it has the opposite appearance. A., serious, was speaking to B. about electric heating: " . . . the heat reaches twenty degrees in a few minutes . . . ," B. responded: " . . . wonderful . . . ," the faces and the voices got lost in the darkness.

I was alone, measuring the extent of the sickness: a tranquillity that wouldn't quit. The excess of the preceding day was useless! Extreme lucidity, stubbornness, happiness (chance) had guided me: *I was in the heart of the castle*, I was living in the house of the dead man and I had passed all bounds.

My thoughts went off in every direction. I was stupid to give things a value they didn't have. This inaccessible castle—inhabited by insanity or death—was a place like any other. *The day before I seemed to be conscious of my game*: it was make-believe, mendacity even.

I could make out the silhouette of the others. They were no longer talking, the night had effaced them. In spite of everything it was my luck to be staying, ill, in the dead man's house: my artful malaise, my poignant cheerfulness—of doubtful authenticity.

At least the bald one was lifeless, *authentically* dead, but what did *authentic* mean?

From the idea he gives of himself, I can't accurately gauge A.'s misery. I imagine a calm reflection, inserting its tedious limpidity in the universe. By these slow labors of action and reflection following one another, by this execution of bold strokes that are basically so may acts of lucid prudence, what can he achieve?

His vices have just one goal according to him: to give his

position a *material* consequence.

"The impostor!" I said to myself at the end of my reflection.

(I was calm and ill.)

Could he really not know that his attempt has the same effrontery as a die?

No one of us is more a *die*, drawing from chance, from the bottom of an abyss, some new derision.

That share of truth which we unquestionably draw from the games of the intellect . . .

How can we deny the depth, the reach of the intellect?

And yet.

The zenith of the intellect is at the same moment its breakdown.

It melts away: what defines man's intelligence is that it escapes him. Seen from the outside, it is only weakness: A. is only a man intoxicated by its possible depth and no one could resist it were it not for the fact that greater depth gives us a superiority (manifest or hidden) over others. The greatest intellect is basically the most easily duped: to think that one apprehends the truth when one is only evading, vainly, the obvious stupidity of *everyone*. And no one really has what each one thinks: something more. A childish belief of the most rigorous ones in their talisman.

What no one before me achieved, I cannot achieve, and striving to, I have only been able to mimic the mistakes of others: I dragged the weight of others along with me. Or better, believing that *I* alone had not succumbed, I was only they, bound by the same shackles, in the same prison.

I succumb: A. and myself, close to B., in a mystical castle . . .

At the banquet of the intellect, the ultimate imposture!

Even the bald one next door—doesn't he have a false rigidity in death?

His image obsesses B. (a corpse separates us).

A wax museum dead man!
Jealous of the dead man! perhaps of death itself!
The idea came to me—sudden, clear, irremediable—that incest linked the dead man to B.

.

I fell asleep and woke up much later.

I was alone.

Unable to satisfy a need, I rang.

I waited. They had left only a dim light and when he opened I didn't recognize Edron at first. He stood before me. His feral eyes stared at me. I stared back at him. The room was immense; he came slowly toward the bed. (But a white jacket is reassuring.)

I simply said to him:

"It's me."

He didn't reply.

To find me lying in bed, *that day*, in B.'s room was beyond his comprehension.

He didn't say a word. He looked like a forester in spite of the jacket, and my defiant attitude was not that of a master. A poor, sick man, let in on the sly, prowling with a corpse's beard, was more in the position of a poacher.

I remember the time he spent in front of me, frozen in an undecided posture (he, the master's man, looked cornered, not knowing what to say nor how to exit . . .).

I couldn't help laughing inside, and I had to painfully calm that laughter: I was suffocating.

Considering that just then the discomfort from which I might have screamed gave me a startling flash of lucidity!

B. often talked to me about Edron and her father, hinting at the unnatural friendship of the two men. It finally became clear to me . . . The background of anguish against which B.'s uncertain boldness, her despondent mirth, her excesses in two contrary directions, licentiousness and submission, stood out—at the same moment I had the key to it all: B. as a little girl, victim of the two monsters (Now I'm sure of it!).

In these circumstances and because of the great calm I was in, I felt the limits of anguish recede. A. stood in the doorway without saying a word (I didn't hear him come): "What have I done," I thought, "to be thrown back like this into the impossible in any case?" My eyes went from the gamekeeper to the clergyman: I imagined the God that the latter denied. In my calm an inner wail, from the depths of my solitude, shattered me. I was *alone*—a wail that no one heard, that no ears will ever hear.

What unimaginable force would my lamentation have had if there were a God?

"Think about it though. Nothing can escape you now. If God doesn't exist, this moan, choked back in your solitude, is the extreme limit of the possible: in this sense there is no element of the universe that is not under its power! It is not subject to anything, it dominates everything and yet is formed out of an infinite awareness of impotence: *out of a sense of the impossible to be exact!*"

Stirred by a kind of joy.
I looked the old man straight in the eyes. I could tell he was wavering inside.

I realized the Father was enjoying himself on the threshold . . .
Motionless (he was enjoying himself at my expense; his cunning ideas, by no means excluding friendship, were lost in indifference), A. remained in that pose for just a few moments.

(He takes me amiably for a fool.
Moreover he makes fun of my "play-acting."
I had no doubt about the bluff of anguish . . .)

At that suspended moment—I had sat up on my bed opposite the gamekeeper, and my life was escaping me in my powerlessness—I thought: "I was cheating in the snow yesterday, it was not the leap that I imagined." This lucidity connected with A.'s presence did not change my state in the least: Edron remained in front of me and he was a man I could not laugh at.

I had thought at first of the big knife he probably had under his jacket (I was sure he had it in fact and I knew he was thinking about it himself but he was paralyzed). Hearing the ring and seeing him walk by, A. was afraid . . . , but he was wrong: it was the forester who gave in.

Confronting him, in the horror I was in, I even experienced a slight sensation of triumph. I had the same feeling with regard to A. (at that moment my lucidity reached exaltation). At the height of fear there was no limit to my joy.

It no longer matters to me that my state, in the eternal absence of God, exceeds the universe itself . . .

The sweetness of death radiated from me; I was sure of a faithfulness. Far beyond Edron and A., B.'s distress approached the plunge that M. had made into death. The gaiety, the frivolity of B. (but I had no doubt that at this very moment she was in the dead man's room *wringing her hands*), was just one more access to nakedness: to the SECRET that the body abandons with the dress.

Until then I had never had that clear awareness of my farce: my whole life making an exhibition of itself and the curiosity I had had to reach the point where I was, where the farce is so complete and so true that it says:
"I am farce."

I saw so far in my passion for seeing.
The haggard, irascible face of the world.
The fine, ludicrous visage of the gamekeeper . . . , I cheerfully brought his ignominy into focus against an inaccessible background . . .
Suddenly I realized that he would walk away, that in due time he would come back, bringing the tea tray.

In the end I made all those connections that link each thing to the other: so that each thing is dead (stripped *naked*).

. . . that SECRET—that the body abandons . . .

B. didn't cry but awkwardly wrung her hands.
. . . the darkness of a garage, a male odor, an odor of death . . .

. . . finally the bald one's inanimate body . . .

I have the naïveté of a child; I say to myself: my anguish is great, I am taken aback (but I had *in my hands* the sweetness of her nakedness: *her awkward* hands being wrung were just the dress raised up, revealing . . . There was no longer any difference between the two and that painful awkwardness linked the cornered nakedness of the little girl to the cheerful nakedness in front of A.).

(Nakedness is only death and the tenderest kisses have an aftertaste of rat.)

PART TWO

DIANUS

*(Notes Drawn from the Notebooks
of Monsignor Alpha)*

. . . not a line where, like the morning dew in the sunshine, the sweetness of anguish does not come into play.

. . . I really ought rather to . . .
. . . but I want to wipe out my footprints . . .

... the senseless attention, analogous to the fear that intoxication can be, to the intoxication that fear can be ...

I'm becoming gloomy and a kind of hostility keeps me in the darkness of the room—and *in this dead silence.*

Since it may be time to answer the riddle that's entered the house like a thief. (Better to answer in my turn by ceasing to live, instead of getting excited like a girl).

Now the water of the lake is black, the forest in the storm is as funereal as the house. It was no use saying to myself, "A dead man in the next room! ... " and smiling at the idea of an entrechat; my nerves are on edge.

A few minutes ago E. went out, haphazardly, into the night: since she was in no condition even to close the door, the wind slammed it.

I wanted to be utterly in command of myself. I fancied that my freedom was complete: and now my heart has sunk. My life has no way out: this world surrounds me with malaise. It begs a grinding of teeth from me.—"Imagine that E., having betrayed you (when you only wanted it physically), now kills herself out of love for a dead man, for D.!"

E. is pining with love for a man who held her in contempt. In his eyes she was nothing but an orgy partner. I don't know if I still have the heart to laugh at her foolishness—or to weep at my own.

No longer being able to think of anything but her, and the dead man, I can't do anything—but wait.

The bitter consolation: that to a life of libertinage E. prefers anguish, wandering at the shore of a lake! I don't know whether she'll kill herself . . .

The last few days, at the thought of my brother dead, even because of the affection I have for him, I imagined it would be hard for me to keep from laughing. But now death is there.

It's odd to be in such agreement, in the deepest part of oneself, with the denial of what one wants and doesn't cease wanting.

Or maybe? I prefer for D. to be dead . . . I would rather that E., wandering in the dark near the lake, no longer hesitated to fall . . . The idea revolts me now . . . : just as the water that would drown her would revolt her.

My brother and I had wanted to live an endless festival up to his death! Such a long year of playfulness! The disconcerting thing was that D. remained open to depression, to shame: he always had a comical temperament, connected, I imagine, with the "infinite interest" given to what surpasses, not just limited being, but the very excesses by which we try to transcend its limits. And myself, now, in the state he has left me in, like a fish on the sand, I remain tense.

At the limit of sleeplessness, of fatigue, to yield to superstition!
Naturally it's curious (but much more distressing) that, cut off by the storm, there is no light at this wake.

The rumbling of the thunder doesn't cease answering to a nauseous feeling of lost possibility. The glimmer of a church candle illuminating a photograph of E., masked, half-naked, dressed for the ball . . . , I don't know any more, I'm here, without recourse, empty like an old man.

"The sky stretches over you, immense and dark, and the dim moonlight through a cloud chased by the wind only blackens the ink of the storm. There is nothing on earth and in the sky, inside you and outside you, that doesn't contribute to your prostration."
—"Here you are about to fall, ungodly priest!" And I start repeating that stupid curse out loud, sneering, at the window.

So *painfully* comical! . . .

After all, the moment of ruin, when you don't know if you're going to laugh or cry, if it weren't for the fatigue, the sensation of musty eyes and mouth, of nerves slowly worn out, has the greatest leaping power. Later at the window (at the moment when the unpredictable light of a lightning flash would reveal the expanse of the lake and the sky), I would like to address God with a false nose on my face.

The infinitely tender sensation of *living*—E., the dead man, and I—a possibility that can't be grasped: the slightly stilted and majestic absurdity of death, something preposterous, mischievous, about the dead body on a bed—like the bird on the branch—there is nothing that isn't suspended, a magic silence . . . , my collusion with D., a whole childish mischievousness, the gruesome ugliness of the grave digger (who doesn't seem to be blind in one eye by chance); E. roaming the water's edge (it's dark inside her; she holds out her hands for fear of knocking against the trees) . . .

. . . a few moments ago, I myself was in the state of empty, inexhaustible horror that I can have no doubt she is in: Oedipus wandering with his eyes torn out . . . and his hands outstretched . . .

. . . an image, at the exact moment, the way a bit of food gets stuck in the throat: E., naked, wearing precisely the false nose with mustache I was thinking of . . . she was at the piano singing a tender love song, the one that suddenly breaks out of tune with a violent:

. . . Ah! come on and put your . . . in my . . .

. . . drunk and overstrained from having sung with a vulgar violence: a stupid smile acknowledged this exhaustion. To the point where one trembles with excitement. Already a slight panting linked us . . .

At this degree of exasperation, love has the rigor of death. E. had the simplicity, the elegance and eager timidity of an animal . . .

But how does one—the electric light having abruptly come back on—keep from feeling the emptiness of insomnia so strongly that one staggers, on seeing written that *gruesome* word, "had" . . .

Her image as a carnival slave . . . and that scanty clothing . . . in the harsh light.
I have never doubted that a day would in fact dawn in me when the unbearable would be there. And the hope never left me, even here, that I would grip the stone hand of the commander.

How theatrical it was, holding the wax candle, to go look, in the returned darkness, at the dead man lying between the flowers, the odor of mock orange mixed with that of death detergent!

My calm resolve, my simple composure responding to an appearance of boundless irony (the indefinable and affected side of the face of dead people), how difficult it is to connect a feeling of faithfulness to one of jealousy and envy! But precisely what helps me endure the unbearable is that utterly dark tenderness which invades me . . .

To the point of, remembering the depression which, after his break with B., made him decide to come end his life at . . . , experiencing the suffocating impression he gave me as an orgasm.

. . . completely, life consisting of the dark tenderness that joins me to D., in the morning twilight—and dawn— atmosphere of an execution . . . : what is neither tender nor dark doesn't touch us. The only annoying factor, at the threshold (but, slowly, I gained control of myself) of an outburst of impotent spite, was this: that D. never reached that degree of hateful friendship, where mutual understanding arises from the certainty that both are blamable.

E. will no longer come back, the clock having struck six . . . Only death is beautiful enough. Crazy enough. And how could we bear this silence without dying? It's possible that no one has ever reached my degree of solitude: I endure it on condition that I write! But since E., in her turn, wanted to die, she would not have been able, of course, to do anything that answers as well to the need which my mood conveys.

D. told me one day, with a laugh, that he was gripped by two obsessions (which made him ill). The first: that in no case could he bless anything (the feelings of gratitude that he had sometimes expressed had later proved to be false). The second: that the ghost of God having vanished and the guardian immensity being absent, it was necessary for him to live an immensity that no longer limited and did not protect. But that element which a feverish search had not been able to attain—a kind of impotence made him tremble—I find in the peacefulness of sorrow (which required his death . . . and that of E . . . : my irremediable solitude). What a man once might have felt to be chilling, but agreeable, in recognizing that a hand pressed against the window pane is that of the devil, I'm experiencing now, letting myself be suffused, and intoxicated, by an unavowable tenderness.

(. . . would I have the courage to laugh about it, or not? . . .)

I literally crawled to the window, faltering like a sick man: the sad light of the dawn, the low sky over the lake, correspond to my state.

All the mediocre qualities that railroad tracks and signals bestow on what, in spite of everything, is located in their domain . . . : my uncontrollable, out-of-the-way laughter is lost in a world of stations, mechanics, workers up at dawn.

So many men and women met in the course of my life who didn't thenceforth cease *for a moment* to live, to think one thing then another, to get up, wash themselves, etc., or to sleep. Unless an accident or some illness withdrew them from the world, in which they left only an unbearable cadaver.

Almost no one avoids, one day or another, the situation that confines me now; no question posed in me that life and life's impossibility have not posed to each of them. But the sun blinds, and even though the blinding light is familiar to all eyes, no one gets lost in it.

I don't know if I will fall, if I will even have the necessary strength in my hand to finish the sentence, but the implacable will prevails: the remains which at this table I am, when I've lost everything and a silence of eternity reigns in the house, are there like a bit of light, which perhaps is falling into ruin, but does radiate.

When the *dark* light into which the certainty of E.'s death had plunged me was replaced by the consciousness of my folly, my malaise—I need now to say it—was miserable. When the gravel of the driveway crunched under E.'s footsteps, I drew back from the window and hid in order to see her: she was the image of weariness. She passed near me slowly, with her arms hanging and her head low. It was raining, by the sad morning light. Was I at the end of things any less than she was after this endless night? It seemed to me that she was making a fool of me: fallen from a high place, I felt ridiculous and my situation combined odiousness with a dead silence.

Yet, if at some moment a human being can say, "Here I am! I have forgotten everything; up to this point it was nothing but phantasmagoria and delusion, but the noise has hushed, and in the silence of tears, I am listening . . . ," how to keep from seeing that that implies this odd feeling: *to be vexed?*

I am different from D. in having that mania for *being able* which raises me up suddenly like a cat. He wept and I dissemble. But if D. and his death did not humiliate me, if I did not experience D., deep within me, *in death*, like a spell and a vexation, I no longer could surrender to passionate impulses. In this humiliated transparency constituted by the distraught but enraptured consciousness of my folly and, through it, of a deathlike emanation, I might finally be able to arm myself with a whip.

That is not the sort of thing that calms the nerves . . .

My misery is that of the devout believer who can't satisfy the unpredictible whim of the god. I went into E.'s room with the whip in the back of my mind, and I came out with my tail down . . . and worse.

A brief glimpse at madness . . .

E. wild-eyed, her teeth clenched by a monotonous curse, muttering this insult and nothing else: "bastard . . . ," in his absence, slowly tearing her dress, as if she had lost the rational use of her hands.

I hear my temples throbbing and the sweetness of my brother's room is going to my head, drunk with the fragrance of the flowers. Even in his moments of "divinity," D. never reached and never communicated this transparency that embalms.

That which life does not radiate, that miserable silence of laughter, veiled in the intimacy of being, death may have— rarely— the power to lay bare.

What is doubtless the bottom of things: a staggering naïveté, a limitless abandon, a drunken exuberance, a vehement "No matter!" . . .

. . . even the Christian's measured infinity defines, by an unfortunate setting of bounds, a power and a need to break them all.

The only way to define the world was to first bring it down to our measure and then, with a *laugh*, to discover it in this: that in fact it is beyond our measure. Christianity finally reveals what truly is, the way a dike at the moment it's breached reveals a force.

How not to be tempted, being moved to dizziness by an uncontrollable impulse inside me, to rebel, to curse, to want at all costs to limit that which cannot be given any limit? How to keep from collapsing, telling myself that everything within me demands that this movement that's killing me come to a stop? And this movement not being unconnected with D.'s death nor with E.'s sorrow, how not to admit it finally: "I cannot bear *that which I am*?" This trembling in one hand, which a few minutes ago I saw armed with a whip, is it not already a wailing in front of the cross?

But if chance changed, this moment of doubt and anguish would make my pleasure doubly intense!

Is it not the key to the human condition that Christianity's having set the necessary limits to life, to the extent that fear placed them too close, is at the origin of anguished eroticism—of the whole erotic infinity?

I cannot even doubt that without the shameful intrusion on E.'s privacy I would not have been *enchanted* next to the dead man: the room, with the flowers, was like a church, and what pierced me with the long knife of ecstasy was not the eternal light, it was the insufferable, and empty, laughter of my brother.

A moment of complicity and intimacy, holding hands with death. A moment of levity on the edge of the abyss. A moment without hope and without an opening.

I know, I only have to give way to the imperceptible slide of trickery: a slight change and I put an eternal stop to what chilled me: I tremble before God. I raise the desire to tremble to infinity!

If human reason (the human limit) is exceeded by the very object to which the limit is given, if E.'s reason succumbs, I can only harmonize with the excess that will destroy me in my turn. But the excess *that burns me* is the harmony of love within me and I don't tremble before God, but with love.

Why did I go, anguished, into the inhuman silence of the forest, in the leaden, oppressive light of massive black clouds, with the ridiculous image of Crime pursued by Justice and Vengeance on my mind? But in the end what I found, in a magical sunbeam and in the flowery solitude of the ruins, was the flight and the entrancing cries of a bird—tiny, mocking, and dressed in the gaudy plumage of a bird of the islands! And I came back holding my breath, bathed in a halo of impossible light, as if the ungraspable, grasped, left me standing on one foot.

As if a dreamlike silence was D., whom an eternal absence would manifest.

I crept back in: struck with enchantment. It seemed to me that this house, which the evening before had stolen my brother, would be blown over by a breath of air. It would steal away like D., leaving behind it an empty space, but more exhilarating than anything in the world.

Went back, once more, into my brother's room.

Death, myself and the house suspended outside the world, in an empty part of space where the diaphanous smell of death intoxicates the senses, tears them and streches them to the point of anguish.

If tomorrow I re-entered a world of easy, sonorous words, I would have to dissemble, as a ghost would have to do, even though it would like to pass for a man.

I had advanced, on tiptoes, not far from E.'s door: I didn't hear anything. I went outside and made my way to the terrace, from which one sees the interior of the room. The window was half-open and I could see her spread out motionless on the carpet, her long body indecently dressed in a black lace corset.

The arms, legs, and hair were radiating in every direction, uncoiled in abandon like the spirals of an octupus. The center of this radiance was not a face turned toward the floor, but the other countenance, deeply cleft, whose nudity was accentuated by the stockings.

The slow rush of pleasure is in one respect the same as that of anguish; that of ecstasy is closely related to both. If I had wanted to beat E., this was not the effect of a voluptuous desire: I've never had the desire to beat except when I was worn out; I believe that only impotence is cruel. But in the state of intoxication that the closeness of death kept me in, I couldn't help sensing an awkward analogy between the *spell* of death and that of nudity. From D.'s lifeless body there emanated a murky feeling of vastness and perhaps because of that lunar immobility, the same was true of E. on the carpet.

Leaning on the balustrade of the terrace I saw one of the legs move: I could tell myself that a dead body might have had that slight reflex. But her death, at that moment, would have added only an imperceptible difference *to what was*. I went down the steps *intoxicated with horror*, not for any definite reason, but under the trees whose leaves still dripped with rain it was as if this unintelligible world were communicating its wet secret of death to me.

In what way are that moan—that sob that welled up without breaking into tears—and that sensation of infinite decay less *desirable* than the happy moments? comparing these moments to those of horror . . . (I picture absurd delights, an apricot pie still warm, a hawthorn bush in the sunshine, humming with the mad buzz of bees).

But I cannot doubt that in my absence E. put on that party outfit before going into the dead man's room. Talking about her life with my brother, she had told me that he liked her scantily dressed in that way.

The idea of her entry into the dead man's room literally wrings my heart . . .
Returning to her senses, she must have broken down sobbing: this image glimpsed in a flash is not that of death, nor of an untenable lasciviousness—it is the distress of a child.

The need of misunderstandings, of misapprehensions, of forks grating on the window pane, everything that a child's despair announces, the way a prophet announced the approach of misfortune . . .

Going by E.'s door again, I didn't have the heart to knock: there was no sound. I have no hope and apprehension of the irremediable gnaws at me. Indeed, I can only desire feebly that, with E. restored to her right mind, life will resume.

The Dominion

Will I allow myself to fall in my turn?
In the long run, writing muddles me.
I am so tired that I dream of a total dissolution.

If I start from any meaning, I exhaust it . . . or eventually I fall upon meaninglessness.

The unexpected splinter of bone: I was chewing heartily! . . .

But how to stop there, dissolved, at meaninglessness? That can't be done. A piece of meaninglessness, and nothing more, opens onto some meaning or other . . .
. . . leaving an aftertaste of ashes, of dementia.
I look at myself in the mirror: circles around the eyes, the dull look of a cigarette butt.

I would like to fall asleep. But seeing, a few minutes ago, E.'s window closed gave me a shock, and being unable to bear it, I remain awake, stretched out on the bed where I write. (Actually, what gnaws at me is my not being able to accept anything. When I saw her on the floor through the open window, I was afraid she had taken some poison. I no longer doubt that she's alive, since the window is closed, but can't stand her either alive or dead. I don't admit that she escapes me, under shelter of closed windows or doors.)

I don't shut myself inside the idea of sorrow. I imagine the freedom of a cloud filling the sky, forming and breaking apart with an unhurried rapidity, drawing the power to invade from unsubstantiality and sunderance. Concerning my sorrowful reflection, which without the extreme anguish would have been ponderous, I can thus tell myself that it grants me, just as I'm about to succumb, the dominion . . .

Epilogue

connected with it. The truth is that between death and the endless renewal of life, one cannot make a distinction: we cling to death like a tree to the earth by a hidden network of roots. But we're comparable to a "moral" tree—which would deny its roots. If we didn't naively draw from the wellspring of suffering, which gives us the insane secret, we could not have the transport of laughter: we would have the opaque visage of calculation. Obscenity is itself only a form of pain, but so "lightly" linked to the sudden outpouring that, of all the pains, it is the richest, the craziest, the most worthy of envy.

It matters little, in the fullness of this movement, that it is ambiguous, now lifting one to the clouds, now leaving one lifeless on the sand. Broken, it will be a poor consolation to imagine that an eternal joy springs from my defeat. Indeed, I have to yield to the evidence: the breakers of joy only take place on one condition: that the ebb of pain be no less dreadful. The doubt born of great sorrows cannot help but illuminate those who enjoy—who can fully know happiness only transfigured, in the dark halo of sorrow. So that reason cannot resolve the ambiguity: extreme happiness is possible only at the moment I doubt it will last; it changes on the contrary into heaviness, from the moment I'm certain of it. Thus we can live sensibly only in a state of ambiguity. There is never a clear-cut difference, for that matter, between sorrow and joy: the awareness of sorrow on the prowl is always present, and even in horror the awareness of possible joy is not entirely suppressed: it is this awareness that adds dizzily to the pain, but by the same token it is what enables one to endure the torments. This lightness of the game is so much a part of the ambiguity of things that we feel contempt for the anxious, if they take things too seriously. The Church's error lies less in its morality and its dogmas than in its confusion of the tragic, which is a game, and the serious, which is the mark of labor. On the other hand, because they didn't have any serious character, those inhuman suffocations from which I had suffered in my dreams, in my sleep, were the favorable pretext for my resolution. Remembering the moment when I was suffocating, the suffering seemed to me to arrange a kind of ruse, without which the trap of thought could not be "set." At the moment, it pleases me to linger over that imaginary sorrow, and connecting it with the absurd expanse of the sky, to find in lightness, in "lack of concern," the essence of a notion of myself and of the world that a leap would be. In a mad, cruel, and ponderous symphony, amusingly performed with my dead brother, the hostile and hard tip of a finger, stuck a short while ago, in my dream, in the small of my back—so cruelly that I would have cried out, but I couldn't utter a sound—was a rage that absolutely should not be but was, was inexorable and "demanded" the freedom of a leap. Everything started from there in a violent transport, propelled by the inflexible cruelty of the finger: there was nothing, in my torment, that was not uprooted, raised to the unbearable pain where one awakens. But when I woke up from that sleep, E. was standing before me, smiling: she wore the same clothing, or rather the same lack of clothes as when she was spread out in her room. I hadn't yet recovered from my dream. With the ease she would have had as a marquise in a crinoline, an indefinable smile, a warm inflection of her voice brought me back immediately to the delight of living: "Would it please the Monsignor?" . . . she said to me. Something coarse, I don't know what, added to the provocation of the costume. But as if she couldn't sustain an act for more than a moment, she let me see the crack, and in a rough voice asked: "You want to make love?"

A stormy, fairy-like gleam of light bathed my room: like an armed, youthful and illuminated Saint George attacking a dragon, she hurled herself at me, but the harm she intended me was to tear off my clothes and she was armed only with a hyena's smile.

PART THREE

THE ORESTEIA

Oresteia
skydew
bagpipes of life

night of spiders
of countless hauntings
inexorable play of tears
o sun in my breast long sword of death

rest alongside my bones
rest you are the lightning
rest viper
rest my heart

the rivers of love turn pink with blood
the winds have ruffled my assassin hair

Chance o pale deity
laugh at the lightning
invisible sun
thundering in the heart
naked chance

chance in long white stockings
chance in a lace nightdress

Ten hundred houses fall
a hundred then a thousand dead
at the window of the clouds.

Belly open
head removed
reflection of long storm clouds
image of immense sky

Higher
than the dark top of the sky
higher
in a mad opening
a trail of light
is the halo of death

I'm hungry for blood
hungry for bloody earth
hungry for fish hungry for rage
hungry for filth hungry for cold

Heart greedy for light
belly sparing of caresses
the sun false the eyes false
words purveyors of the plague

the earth loves cold bodies

Tears of frost
uncertainty of the eyelashes

dead woman's lips
inexpiable teeth

absence of life

nudity of death

Through falsehood, indifference, the chattering of teeth, insane happiness, certainty,

in the bottom of the well, tooth against tooth of death, a tiny particle of dazzling life springs from an accumulation of refuse,

I avoid it, it insists; conjested, in the forehead, a trickle of blood mixes with my tears and bathes my thighs,

tiny particle born of deceit, of shameless avarice,

no less indifferent to itself than the upper reaches of the sky,

and the purity of an executioner, of an explosion cutting off the screams.

I open in myself a theater
where a false sleep is playing
an aimless sham
a disgrace that sickens me

no hope
death
the candle blown out

Meanwhile, I'm reading "The Nights of October," surprised at feeling an incongruity between my cries and my life. At bottom, I am like Gérard de Nerval, happy with cabarets, with trifles (more equivocal?). I remember in Tilly my fondness for the people of the village, when the rains, mud, and cold had ended, the bar viragos handling the bottles, and the noses (the snouts) of the big farm domestics (drunk, muddily shod); at night the rural songs would weep in the common throats; there was the coming and going of carousal, farting, laughter and girls in the courtyard. I was happy to listen to their life, scribbling in my notebook, lying in bed in a dirty (and chilly) room. Not a hint of boredom, happy with the warmth of the cries, with the charm of the songs: their melancholy caught one's throat.

The Temple Roof

The feeling of a decisive fight from which nothing would divert me now. I'm afraid, being certain I will no longer avoid the fight.

Wouldn't the answer be: "that I forget the question?"

It seemed to me yesterday that I spoke to my mirror.
It seemed to me that I saw rather far in the distance as if by lightning flashes a region where anguish has led . . . A feeling introduced by a sentence. I've forgotten the sentence: it was accompanied by a perceptible change, like a trip release cutting the ties.

I perceived a backward movement, as deceptive as that of a supernatural being.
Nothing more detached or more contrary to malevolence.—

I sensed, like a self-reproach, the impossibility of ever annulling my declarations.

As if some intolerable oppression hindered us.

A trembling desire that chance, appearing unexpectedly, but in the uncertainty of the night, imperceptible, be seized nonetheless. And as strong as this desire was, I could not help but observe silence.

Alone in the night, I continued reading, prostrated by that sensation of helplessness.

I read **Bérénice** *straight through (I had never read it). Only a phrase from the preface made me pause: " . . . that majestic sadness which forms the whole pleasure of tragedy." I read, in French, "The Raven." I got up and took some paper. I remember the feverish haste with which I reached the table: yet I was calm.*

I wrote:

a sandstorm
advanced
I cannot say
that in the night
she advanced like a wall turned to dust
or like the draped swirl of a phantom
she said to me
where are you
I had lost you
but I
who had never seen her
shouted in the cold

who are you
crazy woman
and why pretend
not to forget me
at that moment
I heard the earth falling
I ran
through an endless field
I fell
the field also fell
a boundless sob the field and I
fell

starless night
empty a thousand times extinguished
did a cry like that
ever pierce you
a fall as long as that.

At the same time, love was consuming me. I was limited by words. I exhausted myself with love in the void, like being in the presence of a desirable woman who was undressed but inaccessible. Without even being able to express a desire.

Stupor. Impossible to go to bed in spite of the hour and the fatigue. I could have said about myself what Kierkegaard said a hundred years ago: "My head is as empty as a theater in which there has just been a performance."

As I stared into the void before me, a touch—immediately violent, excessive—joined me to that void. I saw that emptiness and saw nothing—but it, the emptiness, embraced me. My body was contracted. It shrank as if it had meant to reduce itself to the size of a point. A lasting fulguration extended from that inner point to the void. I grimaced and I laughed, with my lips parted, my teeth bared.

I throw myself among the dead

The night is my nudity
the stars are my teeth
I throw myself among the dead
dressed in white sunlight

Death dwells in my heart
like a little widow
she sobs she is a coward
I'm afraid
I could vomit

the widow laughs to the skies
and rips the birds to pieces

At my death
the horse teeth of the stars
whinny with laughter I *death*

blank death
moist grave
one-armed sun
the death-toothed gravedigger
effaces me

the raven-winged angel
cries
   glory to thee

I am the emptiness of caskets
and the absence of myself
in the whole universe

the horns of joy
trumpet madly
and the sun's bull's-eye
explodes

death's thunder
fills the universe

too much joy
turns back the fingernails.

I imagine
in the infinite depth
the deserted expanse
different from the sky that I see
no longer containing
those glittering points of light
but sheets of flame
greater than a sky
dazzling like the daybreak

formless abstraction striated with fractures
heap of inanities
of things forgotten
here the subject *I*
there the object universe littered with dead notions
where *I* throw out the rubbish
the impotent gestures
the gasps
the shrill cock-crows of ideas

o manufactured nothingness
in the factory of infinite vanity
like a trunk full of false teeth

I leaning on the trunk
I feel
my desire to vomit desire

o collapse
ecstasy from which I fall
asleep
when I cry out
you who are and will be
when I will be no more
deaf X
giant mallet
crushing my head

The sparkle
the top of the sky
the earth
and me.

My heart spits you out star

incomparable anguish

I laugh but I'm cold

To Be Orestes

The gaming table is the starry night where I fall, cast like the die on a field of fleeting possibilities.
I see no reason to "find fault" with it.

Being a blind fall in the night, I exceed my will in spite of myself (which is only the given *within me); and my fear is the cry of an infinite freedom.*

If I did not exceed nature, in a leap beyond "the static and the given," I would be defined by laws. But nature plays me, *casting me further than herself, beyond the laws, the limits that make* humble people *love her.*

I am the outcome of a game, that which if I were not, would not be, might not be.

Within an immensity, I am a more *exceeding that immensity. My happiness and my very being stem from that excessiveness.*

My stupidity gave its blessing to succoring nature, on her knees before God.

What I am (my drunken laughter and happiness) is nonetheless at stake, handed over to chance, thrown out into the night, chased away like a dog.

The wind of truth responded like a slap to piety's extended cheek.

The heart is human to the extent that it rebels (this means: to be a man is "not to bow down before the law").

A poet doesn't justify—he doesn't accept—nature completely. True poetry is outside laws. But poetry ultimately accepts poetry.

When to accept poetry changes it into its opposite (it becomes the mediator of an acceptance)! I hold back the leap in which I would exceed the universe, I justify the given world, I content myself with it.

Fit myself into what surrounds me, explain myself, or see only a children's fable in my unfathomable night (give myself a physical or mythological image of myself)? No! . . .
I would drop out of the game . . .

I refuse, rebel, but why lose my way. Were I to rave, I would be merely natural.
Poetic delirium has its place in nature. *It justifies nature, consents to embellish it. The refusal belongs to clear consciousness, evaluating whatever occurs to it.*
Clear discrimination of the various possibles, the gift for going to the end of the most distant one, are the province of clear attention. The irrevocable venturing of oneself, the one-way voyage beyond every given require not only that infinite laughter, but also that slow meditation (senseless but through excess).
It is penumbra and uncertainty. Poetry removes one from the

night and the day at the same time. It can neither bring into question nor bring into action this world that binds me.

The menace of it is maintained: nature can annihilate me— reduce me to that which she is, cancel the game that I play further than she—which demands my infinite madness, my infinite gaiety, my infinite alertness.

Relaxation withdraws one from the game—as does an excess of attention. Enthusiasm, the heedless plunge, and calm lucidity are required of the player, until the day when chance releases him—or life does.

I approach poetry: but only to miss it.

In nature's excessive game it makes no difference whether I exceed her or she exceeds herself in me (she is perhaps entirely excess of herself), but, in time, the excess will finally take its place in the order of things (I will die at that moment).

It was necessary, in order to grasp a possible within an evident impossibility, for me to imagine the opposite situation first.

Supposing I wish to reduce myself to the lawful order, I have little chance of succeeding completely: I will err through inconsequence—through defective rigor . . .

In extreme rigor, the exigency of order holds such a great power that it cannot turn back against itself. In the experience of it which devout worshipers (mystics) have, the person of God is placed at the apex of an immoral absurdity: the devout worshiper's love realizes in God—with whom he identifies himself—an excess which if he were to assume it personally would bring him to his knees, demoralized.

The reduction to order fails in any case: formal devotion (devotion without excess) leads to inconsequence. The opposite endeavor has chances, then. It has to use bypaths (laughs, incessant nauseas). There where things are ventured, each element ceaselessly changes into its contrary. God suddenly takes on a "horrible grandeur." Or poetry slips into embellishment. With each effort that I make to grasp it, the object of my anticipation changes into a contrary.

Poetry's luster reveals itself outside the moments which it reaches in a deathlike disorder.

(A common agreement makes an exception of the two authors who added the luster of a failure to that of poetry. Misunderstanding is linked to their names, but both exhausted the sense of poetry that culminates in its opposite, in a feeling of hatred for poetry. Poetry that does not rise to the non-sense of poetry is only the hollowness of poetry, is only beautiful poetry.)

For whom are these serpents . . . ?

The unknown and death . . . without bovine silence, the only kind strong enough on such paths. In that unknown, blind, I succumb (I renounce the reasoned exhaustion of possibles).

Poetry is not a knowledge of oneself, and even less the experience of a remote possible (of that which, before, was not) but rather the simple evocation through words of inaccessible possibilities.

Evocation has the advantage over experience of richness and an endless facility but it distances one from experience (which is essentially paralyzed).

Without the exuberance of evocation, experience would be rational. It begins to emanate from my madness, if the impotence of evocation disgusts me.

Poetry opens the night to desire's excess. In me the night abandoned by the ravages of poetry is the measure of a refusal—of my mad will to exceed the world.—Poetry also exceeded this world, but it could not change me.

My fictitious freedom tightened the constraints of the natural given more than it weakened them. If I had been content with it, in the end I would have yielded to the limit of that given.

I continued to question the world's limit, seeing the wretchedness of anyone who is content with it, and I couldn't bear the facility of fiction for long: I demanded its reality, I became mad.

If I was untruthful I remained in the domain of poetry, of a verbal transcendence of the world. If I persevered in a blind disparagement of the world, my disparagement was false (like the transcendence). In a sense, my accord with the world deepened. But being unable to lie knowingly, I became mad (capable of ignoring the truth). Or no longer knowing how, for myself alone, to act out the farce of a delirium, I became mad again, but inwardly: I experienced the night.

Poetry was simply a detour: through it I escaped the world of discourse, which had become the natural world for me; with poetry I entered a kind of grave where the infinity of the possible was born from the death of the logical world.

Logic on its death bed gave birth to mad riches. But the possible that's evoked is only unreal, the death of the logical world is unreal, everything is shady and fleeting in that relative darkness. I can make light of myself and of others in that darkness: all the real is valueless, every value unreal! Whence that facility and that fatality of equivocations, where I don't know if I am lying or if I am mad. Night's necessity springs from that unhappy situation.

The night could only proceed by way of a detour.
The questioning of all things resulted from the exasperation of a desire, which could not come to bear on the void!

The object of my desire was illusion first of all and could be the void of disillusion *only in the second instance.*

Questioning without desire is formal, immaterial. About it we cannot say, "It's the same thing as man."

Poetry reveals a power of the unknown. But the unknown is only an insignificant void if it is not the object of a desire. Poetry is a middle term, it conceals the known within the unknown: it is the unknown painted in blinding colors, in the image of a sun.

Dazzled by a thousand figures composed of worry, impatience, and love. Now my desire has just one object: the beyond of those thousand figures, and the night.
But in the night, desire tells lies and in this way night ceases to be its object. This existence led by me "in the night" resembles that of the lover at the death of his beloved, of Orestes learning of Hermione's suicide. In the form that night takes, existence cannot recognize "what it anticipated."